THE NATIONAL
V
The Official

BEN NEVIS - SCOTLAND
SCAFELL PIKE - ENGLAND
SNOWDON - WALES

ONE BOOK COVERING 3 MOUNTAINS
**Now including information on the UK's
4th Peak - Slieve Donard - N. Ireland**

AN
ESSENTIAL GUIDE TO
HELP YOU COMPLETE
THE
NATIONAL 3 PEAKS WALK

BRIAN G. SMAILES

Walk Guides   **THE YORKSHIRE DALES TOP TEN**
ISBN 0-9526900-5-5

THE DERBYSHIRE TOP TEN
ISBN 1-903568-03-X

THE COMPLETE ISLE OF WIGHT COASTAL FOOTPATH
ISBN 0-9526900-6-3

ISLE OF WIGHT, NORTH TO SOUTH – EAST TO WEST
ISBN1-903568-07-2

THE SCOTTISH COAST TO COAST WALK
ISBN 0-9526900-8-X

THE YORKSHIRE 3 PEAKS WALK
ISBN 1-903568-22-6

THE YORKSHIRE 3 PEAKS WALK SKETCH MAP & ROUTE GUIDE
ISBN 1-903568-24-4

17 WALKS IN GLEN NEVIS
ISBN1-903568-05-6

THE GREAT GLEN WAY
ISBN 1-903568-13-7

THE LANCASHIRE TRAIL
ISBN 1-903568-10-2

THE LYKE WAKE WALK GUIDE
ISBN 1-903568-14-5

THE 1066 COUNTRY WALK
ISBN 1-903568-00-5

SHORT WALKS IN THE LAKE DISTRICT
ISBN 1-903568-20-X

JOHN O'GROATS TO LANDS END (Walking Guide)
ISBN 1-903568-18-8

Cycling Guides   **LANDS END TO JOHN O'GROATS**
ISBN 1-903568-11-0

MILLENNIUM CYCLE RIDES IN 1066 COUNTRY (EAST SUSSEX)
ISBN 1-903568-04-8

Tourist Guides   **TOURIST GUIDE TO VARADERO, CUBA**
ISBN 1-903568-08-0

EXPLORE – FORT WILLIAM & GLEN NEVIS AREA
ISBN 1-903568-25-0

Family History   **HOW TO TRACE YOUR ANCESTORS** Beginners Guide
ISBN 1-903568-19-6

The above can be obtained from bookshops or direct from the address below.

See web site for further book details.
www.chall-pub.fsnet.co.uk

THE NATIONAL 3 PEAKS WALK
ISBN 1-903568-24-2

Third Edition 2005

CHALLENGE PUBLICATIONS
7, EARLSMERE DRIVE, BARNSLEY. S71 5HH

Nunquam Solivagus

THE AUTHOR
BRIAN SMAILES

Holds the record for the fastest 4 and 5 continuous crossings of the Lyke Wake Walk over the North York Moors. He completed the 210miles over rough terrain on 5 crossings in June 1995 taking 85hours and 50minutes. In 2004 he completed his 49th crossing.

His most recent venture was to walk from John O'Groats to Lands End, completing it in August 2003 in 34 days. In August 2001 he cycled from Lands End to John O`Groats, a journey of over 900miles in 6days 13hours 18minutes. This involved carrying food, clothing and tent, and was completed without support between both ends.

Brian lectures on outdoor pursuit courses and between these travels extensively on walking expeditions and projects around Great Britain.

Long distance running and canoeing are other sports he enjoys, completing 25 marathons and canoeing the Caledonian Canal 3 times.

Having travelled extensively throughout the UK, Europe and the Caribbean, Brian has recently been writing international travel guides to enable the holidaymaker to access the world with ease and enjoy it as much as he does.

Brian lives in Yorkshire and has walked the hills and dales throughout the county. In compiling this 3rd edition of The National 3 Peaks Walk, the route still holds as much pleasure in walking it again as it did the first time he walked it.

ACKNOWLEDGEMENTS

It is with thanks to the following people for assistance, that this book has been published: -
Graham Fish
Chris Barber
Trevor Atkinson
Geoff Whittaker
Pam Smailes
Photographs - Brian Smailes, Geoff Whittaker

First Published 1996
Second Edition 2000
Third Edition 2005
ISBN 1-903568-24-2

Published by Challenge Publications, 7, Earlsmere Drive, Ardsley, Barnsley, S71 5HH.
www.chall-pub.fsnet.co.uk

Printed by Dearne Valley Printers, Wath on Dearne, Rotherham.

The information recorded in this book is believed by the author to be correct at time of publication. No liabilities can be accepted for any inaccuracies found. Anyone using this guide should refer to their map in conjunction with this book. The description of a route used is not evidence of a right of way.

CONTENTS

	Page
Plates	1
3 Peaks Adventure	2
Preface to 3rd Edition	3
Introduction	5
The Challenge	7
Preparation	9
The Body	16
First Aid	17
Hypothermia	19
Mountain Safety	21
The Countryside Code	23
Weather Forecasts	24
Navigation	26
Grid References	29
Glen Nevis Area	30
Ben Nevis Sketch Map	34
Walking Route-Ben Nevis	37
Driving Route to Scafell Pike	46
Scafell Area	49
Scafell Sketch Map	53
Walking Routes - Scafell Pike	54
Driving Route to Snowdon	66
Snowdon Area	69
Snowdon Sketch Map	70
Walking Routes - Snowdon	71
Slieve Donard - Northern Ireland	75
Bad Visibility Descents	77
Support Team	79
Post Walk	81
Useful Information	82
Glossary of Words	92

PLATES

	Plate No
The Author at Ben Nevis 'Trig' Point	Cover
Ben Nevis from Corpach	1
View to the Youth Hostel - Glen Nevis	2
Just Past the Halfway Point	3
View of the Walking Route	4
The Body	5
The Final Push to the Summit	6
Ben Nevis Summit	7
Ben Nevis Triangulation Pillar	8
Wasdale Head Start with the Pike Above	9
The Footbridge Crossing the Beck on Route	10
Wastwater on Route to the Pike	11
Crossing the Beck to the Pike	12
Scafell Pike Ahead	13
Scafell Pike-Extreme Conditions	14
View to Sty Head Tarn	15
The Final Approach to Scafell Pike Summit	16
Llanberis Path	17
Pyg Track, Miners Track and Crib Goch	18
View of Final Section of the Pyg Track	19
View to Llyn Llydaw Reservoir - Snowdon	20
The Steep Ascent to the Monolith	21
View Showing the Pyg Track and Miners Track	22
Snowdon Mountain Railway	23

Three Peaks Adventure

With all our equipment together
And plans that have taken weeks
We are on our way with confidence
To tackle the National Three Peaks
You can climb them in any order
So armed with map, compass and whistle
We are heading North of the border
Travelling to the land of the thistle
The first mountain we have to conquer
To test the fitness of women and men
Is the highest climb of them all
To reach the summit of The Ben
For the route to the top of Ben Nevis
We will be taking the tourist track
This is the easiest route up there
And it won't take long to get back
We will be up and down Ben Nevis
Just see how long that it takes
Before we are back in Fort William
And heading on down to The Lakes
We are now leaving The Ben behind us
Filled with anticipation we are alike
To go and climb the next mountain
And reach the summit of Scafell Pike
For the next stage of our mission
We are leaving from Wasdale Head
It is a quick and scenic route up there
At least that is what has been said
Then with Scafell Pike now completed
And all safely back down to our wagon
We are on the final stage of our journey
Heading down to the land of the dragon
For the route to the summit of Snowdon
We will take the Pyg or the Miners path
And our legs now tired and aching
Will think of a nice soak in a bath
Then all safely back to Pen-y-Pass
There is one thing we must do
That is give a special thank you
To a wonderful back up crew
Then thank God it was safely completed
And it was not just all a dream
But what made it all possible
Was the help of the back up team

Geoff Whittaker

PREFACE TO THE 3rd EDITION

The routes described in this book are written for walkers who either choose to take up the 3 peaks 24 hour challenge or to climb each peak at a more enjoyable leisurely pace. There is no rule that says you must complete the 3 peaks in 24 hours. Peaks can be climbed over days, weeks or years. Trying to do this in 24 hours leads to loss of enjoyment and a higher risk of accidents.

The effort required to complete the National 3 Peaks cannot be under estimated. The lack of proper sleep, food and comfort takes it's toll on people of all ages particularly those in mid life and over, which is the average age of the long distance walker.

"One of the ultimate challenges in the United Kingdom" is how many people describe this 3 peaks walk. Ben Nevis at 1344m, Scafell Pike at 978m and Snowdon at 1085m. The challenge of climbing the 3 highest mountains in Great Britain appeals to many walkers. New in this edition is the information for those who would like to tackle a 4th peak, Slieve Donard in Northern Ireland. This is situated in the Mourne Mountains and is 850m in height, more inside.

This book looks at preparation, walking and driving routes to use on this classic walk. The inclusion in this edition of campsites and B&B's for each area should prove a valuable help.

Sketch maps have been included as a guide to use in conjunction with the relevant map.

The photographs give an accurate representation of the spectacular scenery and the conditions that can be encountered on the 3 peaks walk.

Following the advice given in this book, which includes new and updated information, should enable all walkers to complete the National 3 Peaks Walk in a safe and competent manner.

It gives me great pleasure to present this 3rd edition of The National 3 Peaks Walk to help you fulfil your ambition.

Brian Smailes

INTRODUCTION

The National 3 Peaks of Scotland, England and Wales consist of 26 miles of steep rugged ascents and descents. Weather conditions can play a big part in deciding if you can complete the walk safely. Snow, low cloud or darkness can also be deciding factors, so you need to make careful preparations, looking at weather forecasts and the equipment that will be used for the venture.

This walk should ideally be attempted between June-Oct, the longest day being 21st June. Many people attempt the 3 peaks in June so you may well find car parks full and many other walkers around, therefore it is worth looking at other months like May, or July to September. You can of course walk it at other times of the year with caution. It helps if you walk during the week and not weekends, as car parks are more freely available with generally less congestion.

In times of snow, the danger of overhangs, whiteouts and false ledges can all prove fatal if you are ill-prepared. Carry and know how to use essential equipment. In winter an ice axe and crampons are considered essential.

Once you gain the summit of any of these peaks you have an awesome feeling as you look out over the mountains and probably across the low cloud in the valleys and glens. This leaves a lasting impression on any walker of accomplishment, which cannot be equalled.

There are well defined paths leading to the summits of Ben Nevis and Snowdon. Scafell Pike is slightly different, the paths are not so well defined in places, but care in planning the ascent will help you attain the summit and return safely.

The driving route between each mountain is not complicated. Although a suitable route is shown within, drivers can obviously choose their own route which they may feel is more direct or to avoid road works or other congestion.

THE CHALLENGE

In 24 Hours

Start at Loch Linnhe, Fort William by touching the water at the main ferry terminal beside Crannog Sea Food Restaurant. This is near the main car park. Drive 2½ miles, along Glen Nevis and park at the visitor centre. You now follow the route described to the summit of Ben Nevis.

After completing Ben Nevis, head south to either Wasdale Head or Seathwaite in the Lake District. Walk to the summit of Scafell Pike following one of the set routes. You may save some time by following the route from Seathwaite via the Corridor Route to Scafell Pike, returning to Wasdale Head car park *(plate 9)*. My personal preference is to start and finish at Wasdale Head, which I feel is more straightforward, taking only 2½ hours each way. However many people prefer the other route, which takes longer to ascend!

Once you have completed Scafell Pike, head south to Wales. Park at Pen-y-Pass (charge) or in Llanberis depending on which walking route you choose. Most people prefer to start from Pen-y-Pass. Ascend to the summit of Snowdon following one of the routes described.

Your 3 peaks challenge is complete when you drive to Caernarfon Castle and touch the water at the side of the castle car park.

When attempting this challenge in 24 hours extra care should be taken because of the increased exertion required to complete in the time limit. Exhaustion can overcome you while on the mountain, then when you stop, even for a short while, hypothermia can become a problem very quickly.

Due to the distance involved, driver fatigue is a major cause of accidents especially on the 24 hour challenge.

The Leisurely Alternative

As an alternative to the above challenge the 3 peaks can be walked on 3 individual days, not necessarily consecutive. In choosing this method you will have time to look around Fort William, Keswick, Llanberis or any other of the many tourist attractions on route.

Many people think this walk must be completed in 24 hours, it does not. It is probably a more rewarding experience to take your time and enjoy the once in a lifetime event.

PREPARATION

This walk is not considered long compared with many other walks. Maximum distance on one mountain is 9½ miles, even so if you are not prepared it could lead to problems. In preparing for this walk you need to consider the following:-

FITNESS   FAMILIARISATION
FOOD   EQUIPMENT

FITNESS

The main problems on this walk are the steep, rugged ascents and descents especially on Ben Nevis and Scafell Pike. Because of this there is a lot of pressure on the leg muscles, knees and achilles tendon. This pressure will increase considerably if you are attempting to climb the 3 peaks consecutively.

Exercise should be followed to build up stamina i.e. walking, jogging, cycling and swimming all help to improve fitness for this walk.

Walk at a steady pace when ascending each mountain. This will conserve energy and maintain a steady body heat and release of energy. Some walkers set off at a brisk pace and often become exhausted soon afterwards. The combination of exhaustion and loss of energy can hasten the onset of hypothermia.

FOOD

Food consumed both before you start and while walking can affect your body heat and energy level. High energy food such as bananas, rice, pasta, potato and wholemeal bread are all carbohydrate rich and of benefit. A high intake of these carbohydrates coupled with a balanced diet of protein, for building body and muscle strength, should give you the strength and energy to complete this walk.

FAMILIARISATION

Study your map and familiarise yourself with the route and various landmarks, where possible visit the areas before you walk. An escape route should be planned in case of bad weather or in the event of an emergency (see bad visibility descents).

When studying your map, note where the mountain rescue posts are situated, along with the nearest telephones and areas where shelter can be provided. Look for danger areas e.g. gullies, ledges etc.

EQUIPMENT

Carefully select both personal and safety equipment. Clothing should be capable of keeping you warm and dry. It should protect you from the elements as well as changes in temperature that occur between the foothills and the summit.

Boots

These are an essential item on this walk. A good fitting pair of boots can make the difference between success or failure on any walk. Ankle protection is important especially on the peaks of Ben Nevis and Scafell Pike where large stones and scree can inflict damage very easily. It is appropriate to mention here that toe nails should be cut short before the walk as toes can touch the front of the boots when descending, so doing this should stop you losing your toe nails.

Ideally both leather and fabric boots should be waterproofed before use. Most types of leather boots will need 'breaking-in' before use. Regular waxing will help keep the leather supple. A sewn-in tongue will help prevent water and small stones getting into the boot. Before buying boots always try them on wearing the socks you will use with them. The boots should not be too tight as to cramp your toes likewise not too slack that your feet move around inside.

Socks

These should keep the feet warm and cushion them from any knocks and constant pounding. You can usually buy short, medium or long depending on preference. Whatever your choice they should ideally be approximately 60% wool for good insulating property.

Trousers

Should be loose fitting and ideally made of cotton or a fleece type of material. Cotton trousers will be light to wear, keep you warm and most importantly will dry quickly when wet. Fleece trousers will generally keep you very warm. They are lightweight and can be waterproofed.

Jeans are not suitable for walking as they take a long time to dry when wet and become very heavy. They can also chafe the skin, draw the body heat, so giving you hypothermia, and their insulating property is very low. Do not become one of the jeans and t-shirt brigade.

Hat

Much of the body's heat is lost through the head, so some protection is strongly advised.

Jacket

There is a vast assortment of jackets available for this type of venture from fleece to coated materials that are often breathable. If there is a hood attached with a drawstring this will give good protection around the head. Full length two-way zips help to regulate body heat as well as allowing for ease in putting on/taking off while out in a harsh environment.

The addition of numerous pockets, some zipped, provides space for any small items you may like to carry. It is especially beneficial to have a map pocket on the inside. Most types of jackets are washable and can be re-waterproofed to withstand the elements for at least a few hours.

Waterproofs/Windproofs

Jackets that are breathable, waterproof and windproof are popular, but whichever jacket you are buying make sure it is waterproof and not just showerproof.

Some features to look for on waterproof jackets are:-

• Full length two-way zip to help regulate body heat and with putting on/taking off. It should also have a flap over it.

• Side pockets also with a flap over to stop water entering.

• Elasticated or adjustable cuffs are essential to stop the wind flow through the jacket.

When buying your jacket make allowance for the other items of clothing you would normally wear underneath and indeed extra clothing for cold weather.

Waterproof trousers should have an elasticated waist and/or draw-string. Zips on the lower legs are very beneficial as they enable you to put them on/take off without taking your boots off.

Finally all seams on jackets and trousers should be taped to ensure no water passes through. A little candle wax rubbed on the zips will help to keep them running smoothly and keep water out.

Do not wear water/windproofs that are not breathable any longer than necessary as quite often condensation builds up inside. Try to keep the jacket ventilated as much as possible to reduce the condensation.

Breatheable Clothing

Generally clothing which is classed as breathable is only breathable as long as the pores of the item are not blocked, e.g. when wet!

Gaiters

Help to protect the lower leg from the wet or abrasive rock. When walking the routes detailed in this book, I find there is not a great need to wear them. Gaiters should be waterproof, ideally breathable, have a hook to attach them to the boots and a full length zip or velcro fastening to enable you to fit them easily.

Gloves

A pair of fleece, woollen gloves or mittens is strongly recommended when ascending the peaks. You will find that 5 finger gloves, as opposed to mittens, are probably better, especially in gale force winds when handling map and adjusting compass and clothing.

Rucksack

This should be large enough to hold all your personal and safety equipment described. It should be robust enough to stand the test of putting on and removing in all weathers. A rucksack should ideally have wide padded shoulder straps and a waist belt to stop it moving around. It is advisable to put a liner inside to keep items dry in very wet conditions. Most rucksacks have a number of external zipped pockets in which to put small or fre-quently needed items i.e. water bottle, map, food etc.

CLOTHING

Clothing should be built up in layers where warm air can be trapped between each one. Three thin sweaters are more effective than one thick one. If you are hot you can easily take a layer off.

EMERGENCY EQUIPMENT

This includes spare clothing e.g. sweater, socks etc. which should be carried in the rucksack.

Torch

Each person should carry one, take spare batteries and a bulb. Check it works before each mountain.

Pencil & Notebook

It may be necessary to take notes on route especially and in an emergency when positions, names, injuries etc. should be written and passed on to emergency services.

Whistle

Each person should carry a plastic whistle (metal ones can freeze in cold) and they should also be familiar with the 'S.O.S.' signal to alert others in times of emergency.

Survival Bag

Usually made of heavy duty polythene and designed for a walker to get inside to protect them from the harsh environment and to preserve body heat. It is a piece of safety equipment that may never be used but should always be carried.

THE BODY

RUCKSACK
Containing food, drinks, first aid, and clothing, map and compass.

THE HEAD
Should be kept warm, more heat is lost from the head than anywhere else.

THE BODY
Should be kept warm.
Build clothes up in layers with wind/waterproofs on top.

HANDS
Should be kept warm with gloves.

MAIN BODY CORE
Temperature must be maintained.

LEGS
It is important not to wear jeans

ANKLES
Should be protected by wearing boots. These will help stop you going over on your ankle and strengthen it.

FEET
Should be kept well cushioned and dry if possible. Good fitting boots will help prevent blisters

Plate 5

FIRST AID

A knowledge of basic first aid would be helpful on any walk. To be able to bandage cracked ribs, put a sling on or dress a wound can be vital in times of accidents especially on the peaks when hypothermia can set in.

In any accident or emergency situation the ability to reassure the casualty and comfort them is very important, do not move the casualty if the accident is of a possible serious nature e.g. a back or head injury. Keep the casualty warm and reassured, then send for help. Someone should stay with the injured person. If the injury is not of a serious nature the injured person should, if and when possible, be removed from danger.

The possibility of shock or delayed shock can present further problems for the casualty so reassurance and company is vital as well as getting down the mountain to safety.

It is a fact that the majority of accidents happen on the return or second half of the journey. This is probably due to fatigue, cold, tiredness or complacency. Be aware and alert throughout the walk to possible dangers.

Common Types of Injuries

Cuts and grazes   *Broken Arms/Legs*
Blisters   *Cracked Ribs*
Hypothermia   *Head Injuries*
Sprained Ankle/Wrist   *Gashed Shins*
Toe nails dropping off - cut before you go!

All the above, however minor, can prove fatal with the casualty going into shock, especially on an exposed area of the mountain or in times of panic, fog or adverse conditions, coupled with the injury.

Walk in small groups of 4-6 people where possible and be aware. If anyone is badly injured then 2 people should go for help, this should be the fittest person and the best navigator. They should take their own personal safety equipment with them. The rest of the group should stay with the injured person to help and reassure them.

On all three mountains you may encounter midges, especially on Ben Nevis and in the glen there. **Ensure you have an ample supply of midge repellent** so your day is not ruined with midge bites.

Individual First Aid Kit

Adhesive Dressings *Waterproof Container*
Triangular Bandage *Sterile Dressing*
Bandage *Crepe Bandage*
Safety Pins *Gauze/Lint*
Scissors *Micropore*
Insect Repellent *Sun Cream*

Leaders First Aid Kit

A leaders first aid kit is available from outdoor shops and is recommended for group walks.

HYPOTHERMIA

Hypothermia is caused when the body core temperature falls below 35°C. If a walker is not properly prepared for the conditions *(plate 5)* or the equipment/clothing is not satisfactory then a combination of the cold, wet, exhaustion and the wind chill factor can give a walker hypothermia.

The Signs and Symptoms in Descending Order:-

Shivering
Cold, pale and dry skin
Low body temperature
Irrational behaviour
A gradual slip into unconsciousness
Pulse and respiratory rate slow
Difficulty in detecting breathing and pulse when unconscious
Death

Ways of Preventing Hypothermia

1. Build up body clothing in thin layers, adding on or taking off as necessary.
2. Have suitable wind/waterproofs with you.
3. Take some food/hot drink or boiled sweets which produce energy and heat during digestion.
4. Wear a balaclava/woolly hat to insulate the head, and some gloves *(plate 5)*.
5. Shelter out of the wind.
6. Take a survival bag and if conditions dictate, use it.

In any type of emergency/accident situation it is always advisable to come off the mountain as soon as possible especially in low cloud, snow or other bad conditions. The temperature difference between the valley and the summit can be several degrees. If the injured walker is able to move safely, going down the mountain is usually the best solution.

When conditions do not permit movement and if you are in a sheltered area, stay where you are until such time as conditions improve. It may be at this time that you put on extra clothing and use survival bags.

Treatment for Hypothermia

1. Provide extra clothing and shelter from the elements.
2. Bodily warmth of others helps in a gradual warming.
3. If well enough come down into a warmer sheltered area.
4. Give hot drinks if conscious.
5. Give chocolate or sweets if the patient can still take food.
6. The casualty should be placed so that the head is slightly lower than the body.

DO NOT *rub the skin or use a hot water bottle as this can cause a surge of blood from the central body core to the surface, this could prove fatal.*

Alcohol should not be consumed on any walk and should not be given to anyone who has hypothermia. The body temperature will be lowered as well as giving a false sense of security.

MOUNTAIN SAFETY

Details of your route should be left with your support team or someone who can monitor your progress and most importantly alert the rescue services if you are overdue. Because you plan a route it does not mean you have to use it. It is better to cancel if there is a problem than to risk lives ascending a mountain in atrocious conditions or badly prepared.

Many people do not realise that a calm sunny day in the valley can mean low cloud and gale force winds on the summit, add to this the wind chill factor and a badly prepared walker has got problems *(plate 14)*. Bad weather can sweep in quickly.

Only walk routes which are within the capability of your party. One of the most common problems that can lead to accidents is walkers becoming separated from each other. There should be a party leader and that person should ensure the group walks at a sensible pace. This is usually the speed of the slowest walker. Each person should carry a map and compass and know how to use them. A route card should be carried by each person and they should all have been involved in drawing up the route before hand.

If you are delayed e.g. you have descended into the wrong valley, inform your base or the police as quickly as possible to avoid the mountain rescue team from being called out unnecessarily.

All walkers should be familiar with the
INTERNATIONAL DISTRESS SIGNAL

- 6 long blasts on whistle
- 6 shouts or waves of handkerchief
- 6 flashes of torch in succession

All followed by a pause of one minute, then repeated.

A red flare is a distress signal.

You may at some time have to pass on an emergency message to police. You should have all the information written down to help ensure the right details are passed on to the emergency services.

These are:-
- Name and age of casualty
- Nature of injuries
- Location with 6 figure grid reference and description of area around them
- Time of accident
- Details of the rest of the party with colours of clothing worn
- Where you are calling from and your name and address

The Mountain Code

- Select equipment carefully
- Learn how to use it
- Be physically fit
- Know how to use a map and compass
- Where possible make an early start allowing time later in the day for bad weather
- If possible plan an alternative route for bad weather
- Keep together
- Fill in route card and give a copy to the support team.
- Check weather forecast

THE COUNTRYSIDE CODE

The countryside is a place where many people like to escape to and enjoy at various times. To do this we need to look after it when we use it and to preserve it for future generations.

The following is a simple lists of do's and dont's to help everyone enjoy the countryside.

Do
- Guard against all risk of fire
- Leave gates and property as you find them
- Keep dogs under close control
- Use gates and stiles to cross walls and fences
- Protect wildlife, trees and plants
- Take litter home
- Leave nothing but footprints, take nothing but photographs
- Be conscious at all times of erosion of footpaths
- Consider other people

Don't
- Play radios etc. or create unnecessary noise
- Take mountain bikes on walkways
- Touch machinery, livestock or crops

WEATHER FORECASTS

The importance of predicting the weather pattern before you ascend each peak can be vital to the success or failure of you and your team.

Notices displaying the current weather patterns on the peaks of Ben Nevis and Snowdon are usually near the start of the routes described. It is advisable to listen to the forecast on local radio if possible for the area you are in.

Calm, still weather in the valley or glen can turn to gale force winds on the peaks. Check your forecast before you ascend, are you liable to encounter low cloud, heavy rain, snow or scorching sun on your journey? Usually the forecast can help in deciding what and how much extra clothing you need to take with you and equally whether you need sun cream, insect repellent and extra fluid.

It is essential not only to listen to the forecast but also to write it down and remember it. You can then plan your day to make the best use of the wind walking with the wind behind you.

When walking in mountainous country you can often tell if there is or will be a deterioration in the weather by the onset of low cloud around the peaks. Before this happens check your present position and look in the direction you are intending to go as far as you can see. Take a bearing with your compass then follow that bearing through the cloud to your intended destination using both map and compass where necessary. Never be caught unawares, when you reach that spot look again as far as you can see, take your bearing again then proceed as before.

On the National 3 Peaks, snow can present problems at certain times of the year *(plate 8)*. Whiteout conditions are created by 'driving' snow. Where conditions are very bad then only those with a great amount of experience should be on the mountains. In virtually every type of situation like this it is better to abandon the attempt than to risk lives on dangerous peaks.

NAVIGATION

The ability to find your way from one place to another especially in bad weather is something that needs to be learned. Although we may have a sixth sense or sense of direction, when the fog closes in even the best of us can get lost quickly.

Before embarking on your 3 Peaks Walk you should have an understanding of the basic principles of map reading and compass use. It is not intended that this walking guide should give you the information on how to use navigational equipment but only to point out the need for walkers to be prepared before venturing out especially in bad visibility.

Learning how to read the contours of a map as well as being able to recognise landmarks can only be of benefit. Combine this with basic course plotting and magnetic variation to help you to come down from the mountain in any problem situation.

There is a need to practice your navigation skills until you feel confident enough to venture onto the hills and moorland. Most people know the general principles of pilotage where the sun rises in the east and sets in the west, you can therefore get some idea on a clear day as to which general direction you are walking in, however you would not know if you were heading into danger e.g. steep gullies, cliffs or overhangs.

There are many books that deal with map and compass training, courses are available to those that seek them. Use and learn as much as possible about map and compass work.

Over recent years the use of hand help GPS systems has become much more widespread. They are very useful for pinpointing your position, particularly in bad weather. I strongly recommend them. If taking one on your 3 peaks venture, take some spare batteries.

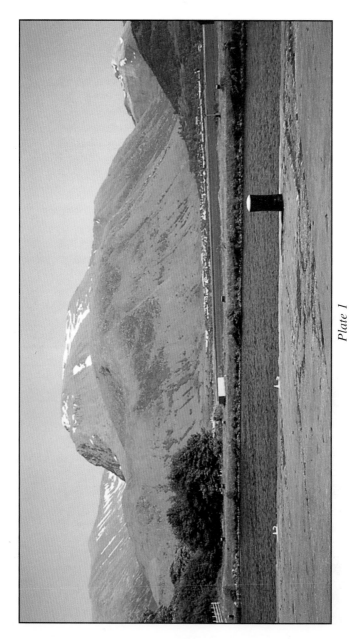

Plate 1
Ben Nevis as viewed from Corpach - Snow on the summit can last into July.

Plate 2
Looking towards Glen Nevis, the start from the Youth Hostel can be seen.
The alternative path can be seen mid right joining the main path up from the Youth Hostel.

GRID REFERENCES

You may find it necessary at some time to either find a place from a given grid reference or to make a grid reference from a place on a map.

All maps have grid lines running north/south and east/west. These are called 'Eastings' and 'Northings' and these lines have numbers on them. They can be further split into tenths, the numbers range from 00 to 99.

Grid references are normally given in six figures. The first three figures indicate how far to the east the place is. The second three figures indicate how far to the north the place is.

To make a grid reference look from left to right on your map. Read the numbers going from left to right. Write down the numbers for the grid line to the left of your position, estimate the tenths to your position and write that number down to make 3 numbers.

Now look up your map and write the 2 numbers from the line just below your position. Repeat the second sequence as above. You should now have 6 numbers usually written as G.R. 647556.

In using this method you should be able to pinpoint your target or position quite accurately on a 1:25000 scale map. Before you ascend the peaks you need to practise until you can both find grid reference points on a map and create a grid reference from a given position e.g. the grid reference for Ben Nevis is 167713 at the 'trig' point using 6 figures, and on O.S. Explorer map 392 Ben Nevis & Fort William.

GLEN NEVIS AREA

Fort William is the main town near the foothills of Ben Nevis. It also represents the start or end of the Caledonian Canal, which runs to Inverness on the east coast *(plate 1)*. The West Highland Way ends here and The Great Glen Way starts here.

Within the area there are many outdoor activity centres which cover all manner of water sports and land based activities.

A tourist information centre in Fort William provides interesting displays of local attractions as well as general information about the area. The Glen Nevis Visitor Centre also gives information, especially on Ben Nevis and Glen Nevis area.

There are many mountains to walk in the area, whisky distilleries to visit, cable cars and cruises to venture on. Local restaurants around Fort William offer good food.

Many of the buildings are stone built and the town is clean and pleasant. The local people are keen to welcome visitors and there are numerous hostelries in which to sample local ale. A visit to the town is not to be missed. There are a number of outdoor shops selling maps, compasses and most outdoor equipment.

Loch Linnhe borders Fort William and provides good fishing and sailing for those who enjoy alternative sports and hobbies. Those walkers who have time to relax after climbing Ben Nevis will find the area around Fort William very pleasant and picturesque.

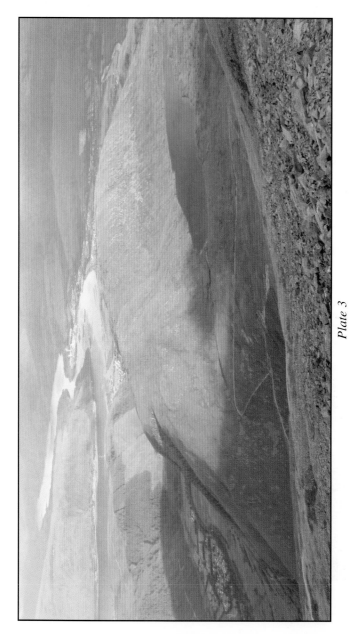

Plate 3
View of Lochan Meall an t Suidhe showing route in foreground.

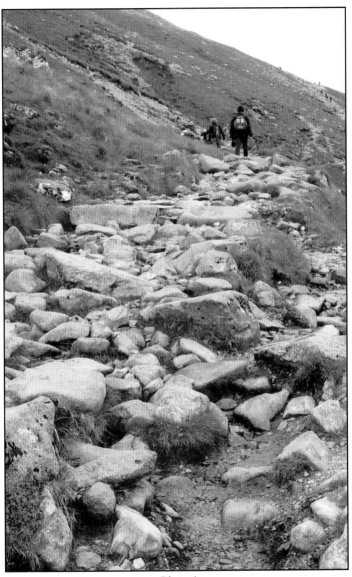

Plate 4
View showing the difficult walking route on Ben Nevis

Over recent years the area has become a set for film producers with films like Braveheart, Harry Potter and Highlander being filmed here.

Travelling to Fort William by car will give some of the best views anywhere in the U.K. particularly travelling through Glen Coe. A rail and bus link will also transport you there from throughout the British Isles. Take a camera to give you some lasting memories.

The path to the summit of Ben Nevis was originally built as a pony track to service the observatory and the hotel which are now in ruins *(plate 7)*. The observatory was operational between 1883-1904. Surprisingly there have been a number of cars that have actually driven to the summit, no doubt with a lot of help. The highest war memorial in Britain is also situated on this summit. The views from here are breathtaking in all directions.

The tourist path is used for the Ben Nevis annual race which usually takes place on the first Saturday in September. It is supervised by the Lochaber mountain rescue team.

The road along Glen Nevis runs for approximately 7 miles. You will find the Visitor Centre, the Glen Nevis Caravan & Camping Park and the youth hostel along this road. The mountains tower on both sides of the glen where the road eventually stops at a car park at the far end.

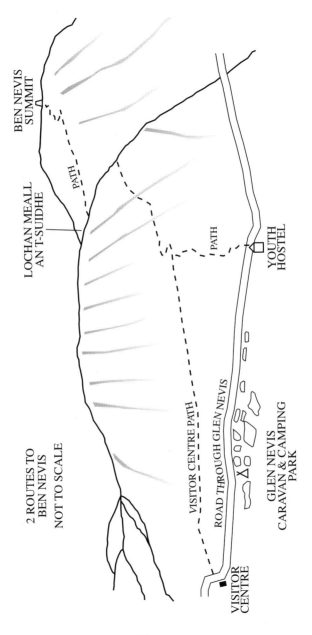

2 ROUTES TO
BEN NEVIS
NOT TO SCALE

BEN NEVIS
SUMMIT

LOCHAN MEALL
AN T-SUIDHE

PATH

PATH

YOUTH
HOSTEL

VISITOR CENTRE PATH

ROAD THROUGH GLEN NEVIS

GLEN NEVIS
CARAVAN & CAMPING
PARK

VISITOR
CENTRE

Plate 6
The final push to the summit of Ben Nevis

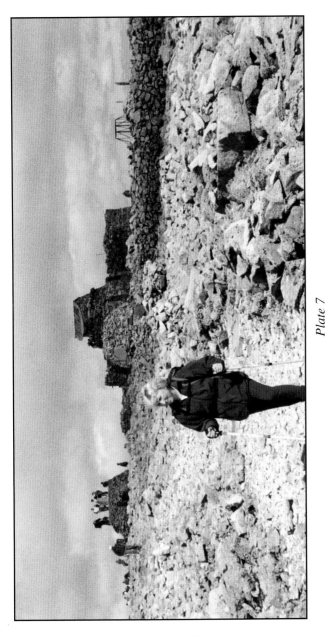

Plate 7

Ben Nevis summit showing the emergency shelter, triangulation pillar and the ruins of the observatory. (Summer conditions)

BEN NEVIS

There are 2 main starting points to climb Ben Nevis -
Glen Nevis Visitor Centre.
The Youth Hostel

Start A - Glen Nevis Visitor Centre

Start by touching the water of Loch Linnhe beside
Crannog Sea Food Restaurant, near the main car
park in Fort William. It is also the main ferry terminal. Take the Inverness road then at the sign to Glen
Nevis at the Nevis Bridge roundabout go straight
across. From the roundabout it is 1.2miles to the
Glen Nevis Visitor Centre. **Park in the free car
park here.** Near the car park is a pedestrian suspen-
sion bridge crossing the River Nevis. Follow this,
passing a guest house on the far side. The visitor centre is now opposite. A sign states 'Ben Path', going
over 3 wooden steps. Ascend for 150m then over 2
steps, going straight ahead. As you ascend you have
a good view of Glen Nevis Caravan & Camping Park
behind you. The path is stony, uneven and ascends
steeply. Continue on this path, which eventually
joins path 'B'.

Start B - Youth Hostel

Start by touching the water as 'A'. Take the Inverness
road, a sign at the Nevis Bridge roundabout points
across to Glen Nevis. Pass Glen Nevis Caravan and
Camping Park and park opposite the youth hostel
400yds further along the road (limited parking). This is
2.1miles from the roundabout.

Your ascent of Ben Nevis begins here *(plate 2)*.
Immediately opposite the youth hostel there is a footbridge, cross it, then cross some steps over a fence.

2 ROUTES TO BEN NEVIS

NOT TO SCALE

ROAD

ROAD

BRIDGE

VISITOR CENTRE

NEVIS CAMPING PARK

YOUTH HOSTEL

PATH

TOURIST PATH

MAIN PATH

RIVER NEVIS

ROAD

NEVIS FOREST

LOCHAN MEALL AN T-SUIDHE

ROCK FORMATION

CARN DEARG 1020

MAIN PATH

ROCK FORMATIONS

CARN DEARG 1214

MOUNTAIN RESCUE POST

ROCK OUTCROP

SHELTER

BEN NEVIS SUMMIT 1344

OBSERVATION RUIN

38

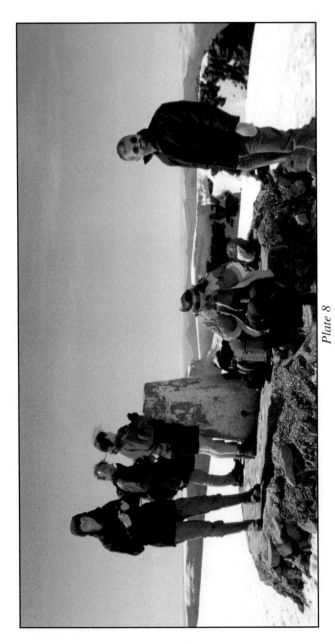

Plate 8
Ben Nevis - The Triangulation Pillar and the roof of Great Britain.
Note - The snow overhang and gully, mid-right.

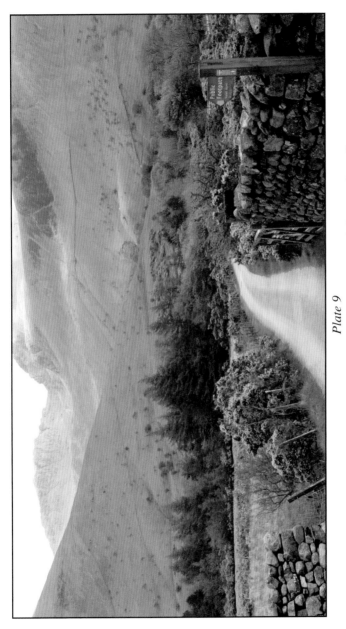

Plate 9
Scafell Pike top left with the route along the road then up the valley.

A sign here usually displays a description of Ben Nevis with the current weather forecast and other information

Continue up a winding, stony path, a man made path develops forming steps as you ascend. Part way up, the path joins path 'A' *(plate 2)*.

Both paths converge and you cross over a wooden platform bridge. You are now on the main path ascending Ben Nevis which is known as "The Tourist Route". The path is very stony and more uneven on this section. Approximately 80m further up is a seat on a bend in the path. You come to a metal bridge and this point affords good views of Glen Nevis.

Cross over a small burn running down a gully, the path here is hard mud, interspersed with stones as it winds up the hillside. The path turns sharp left then right, followed by steps up a steep rock outcrop. A metal bridge spans a gully, again there are good views. The sound of a fast flowing burn running down another gully can be heard. A natural spring escapes from the hillside so the path is usually wet here.

A stone outcrop and another metal bridge with a waterfall beneath is crossed. The path then ascends steeply. You ascend between the two mountains with a burn on your right. It is called Red Burn in English. While ascending the side of the mountain burn you come to a sign saying Conservation Area. The path twists left and right as you approach the loch halfway up the mountain. The path levels out a little here with springs and melting snow making it wet in places. The area is open with a large expanse of grass. Lochan Meall an t-Suidhe is on the left *(plate 3)*.

Follow the path as it turns right and uphill again *(plate 4)*. Some piles of stones and a section of wall mark the path. Go immediately right there. It is important to note that the path going straight on leads to the area climbers use.

Cross a small stream which runs down the path. There are good views over the other mountains. There are some steep drops off to your right. Cross over another burn where walkers usually stop for refreshment. Approaching the summit you can see down the glen to the youth hostel. Loch Linnhe is in the distance *(plate 6)*.

The final ascent is very rocky and uneven, with loose stone and scree. As you approach a gully the route bends sharp right on the scree path. Near the summit the path levels out, with a lot of small stones. Quite often, up to mid summer, this area is covered in snow.

You should see piles of stones on your ascent as you proceed, if there is no snow. Follow your path carefully if there is snow, it is important to stay on the path.

Immediately before the summit take extreme care of the sheer drops over the edge of the mountain, down the infamous Gardyloo Gully, Tower Gully and No.2 Gully *(plate 8)*. Stay on the path watching for snow overhangs, which can be deceiving *(plate 8)*. The gully just before the flat plateau summit is close to the path, so keep right, heading for the ruins of the observatory *(plate 7)*, which date back to Victorian times.

Plate 10
Near the start with the wooden footbridge in the centre.

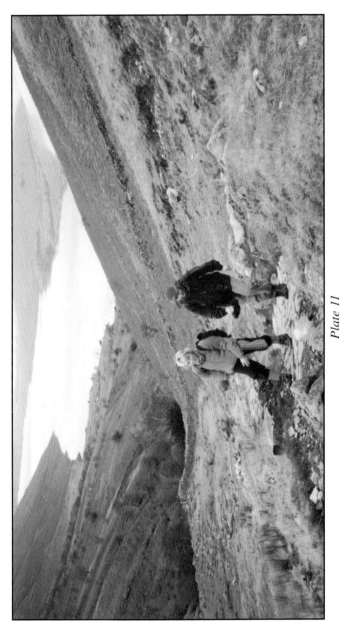

Plate 11
Walkers on route to Scafell Pike with Wastwater in the background. Note: the stony and uneven path.

On reaching the summit you have excellent views in all directions (cloud permitting). There is a triangulation pillar, number S1595 *(plate 8)* and emergency shelter *(plate 7)*. A cross with a cairn and plaque states it is Britain's highest war memorial. It is the Fort William Dudley/Worcestershire Cairn of Remembrance.

After resting for a short time on the summit you may find the cold penetrating the body. This is now the time to start your descent to warmer and more sheltered areas. Retrace your steps down the mountain following the route you ascended.

In times of bad visibility follow the bearings and directions given in the chapter on bad visibility descents. N.B. Ben Nevis should be treated with respect at all times, at over 4,000ft the weather on top can be very different to what you expect e.g. deep snow in May *(plate 8)*, thick fog and ice. It is advisable to carry good quality maps of Ben Nevis with bad visibility routes in scales of 1:10,000 or better. This is for your safety and that of others.

DRIVING ROUTE TO SCAFELL PIKE

	Road	Destination
Leave Fort William	**A82**	North Ballachulish
at North Ballachulish	**A82**	Crianlarich via Rannoch Moor
at Crianlarich	**A82**	Tarbet
at Tarbet	**A82**	Dumbarton
at Dumbarton	**A82**	Erskine Toll Bridge
at Erskine Toll Bridge	**M898**	Glasgow
at Bridge (south)	**M8**	M74
on M74	**M74**	Abington
at Abington	**A74M**	Gretna
at Gretna	**A74**	Carlisle
at Carlisle *	**M6**	Penrith
at Penrith	**A66**	Keswick
at Keswick	**B5289**	Grange
at Grange	**B5289**	Seatoller
at Seatoller	**Minor**	Seathwaite
Leave Walkers	**Drive to Wasdale Head for pick-up**	
at Seathwaite	**B5289**	Crummock Water
at Crummock Water	**B5289**	Brackenthwaite
at Brackenthwaite	**Minor**	Mockerkin Tarn A5086
Mockerkin Tarn	**A5086**	Egremont
at Egremont	**A595**	Gosforth
at Gosforth	**Minor**	Wellington
at Wellington	**Minor**	Wastwater
at Wastwater	**Minor**	Wasdale Head

Route from Carlisle direct to Wastwater

* at Carlisle	**A595**	Cockermouth
near Cockermouth	**A5086**	Egremont
at Egremont	**A595**	Gosforth

at Gosforth turn left onto minor roads to Wasdale Head.

Park in car park on left, just past the northern end of Wastwater or turn right over the bridge into the National trust car park at the side of the campsite (charge).

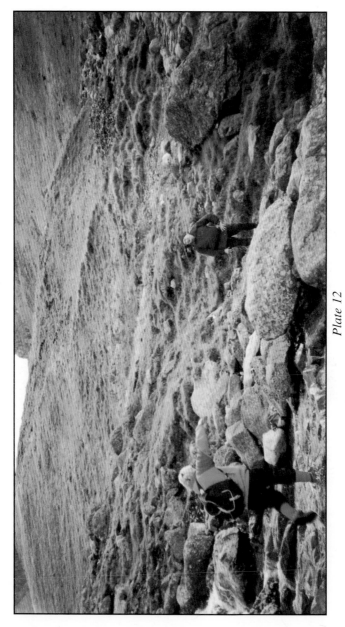

Plate 12
Crossing the beck with Brown Tongue, centre, Scafell Pike, top and walkers path extreme right.

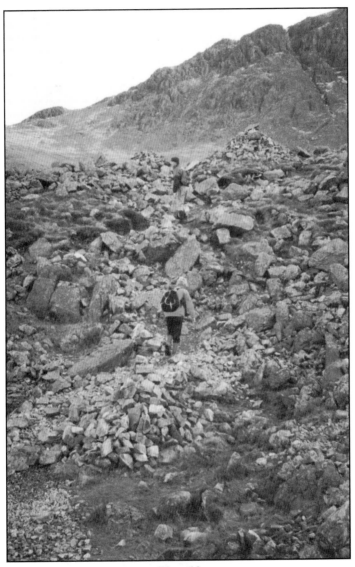

Plate 13
Scafell Pike ahead, walk around the rock outcrop on the left
of the Pike then ascend.

SCAFELL AREA

Scafell Pike is bordered by Wastwater on the south western side of the Lake District and Derwentwater to the north. The nearest main towns are situated several miles away, Keswick, Cockermouth and Ambleside are all within easy reach by car.

There are numerous small villages all round the area with the occasional shop or public house. Picnic areas abound throughout the Lake District especially around the lakes themselves. Birds and other wildlife are plentiful. Scafell Pike is in the heart of the largest national park in England which has 16 lakes within it's area. Much of the area is owned by the National Trust.

When ascending Scafell Pike from Seathwaite via the Corridor Route, ample parking can be found in Seathwaite. You arrive there by passing Grange at the southern end of Derwentwater. There is a café at Seathwaite and a trout farm. The scenery all around the area is very picturesque.

Approaching Scafell foothills from Wastwater there is a small car park on the left and a large National Trust car park (charge) over the small bridge on your right *(plate 9)*, alongside a campsite at the northern end of the lake. Here is the start of the walk. Continuing up the road to where it ends one mile further on past the end of the lake you will find Wasdale Head Hotel. Next to it is an outdoor shop, which has a small campsite opposite it. All around here is mountainous with spectacular scenery.

On the final approach to the summit of Scafell Pike you will see Great Gable with Sty Head Tarn below and Derwent Water in the distance *(plate 15)*. This is the general direction of the Corridor Route. Looking the opposite way you see Wastwater down in the valley. During darkness you can often see Wastwater and it's reflection. This will give you an unmistakable point to aim for on your descent during darkness. Take care to pick out your path carefully on a night descent. The route from Wasdale up to the summit during darkness is by far the easiest to walk and navigate, but leaving the summit in darkness or low cloud and descending off the pike itself can be a lot more difficult.

The first sections of the walk from Seathwaite via the Corridor Route to the summit are good but it becomes progressively more difficult as you proceed.

Whichever route you choose pick out your path carefully, use your map and compass wisely and accurately.

Take your waterproofs with you when visiting Seathwaite. ***This was once the wettest place in Great Britain, now superseded by Fort William!***

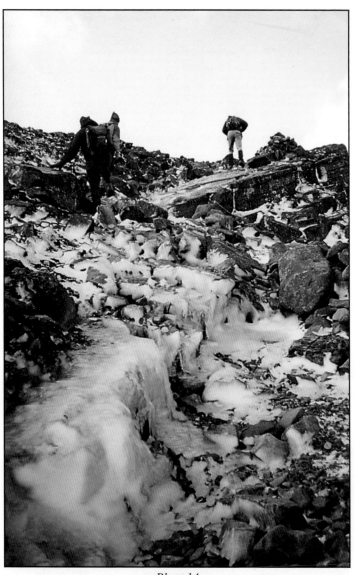

Plate 14
Scafell Pike - Extreme conditions just off the summit.
Wind chill factor -12°C.

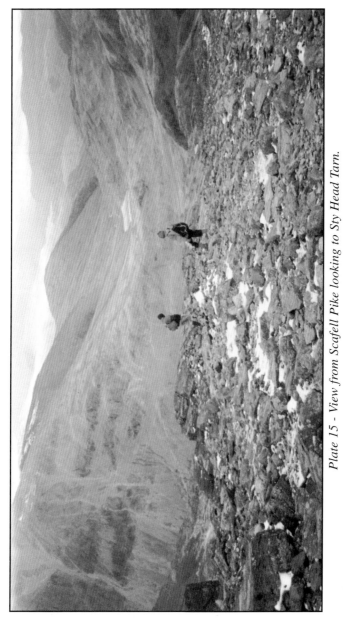

Plate 15 - View from Scafell Pike looking to Sty Head Tarn.
The path leading back to Seathwaite is just visible beyond the tarn. Derwent Water is in centre background.

TO
SEATHWAITE

KIRK FELL

GREAT
GABLE
899m

CORRIDOR ROUTE

STYHEAD GILL

MOSEDALE BECK

STYHEAD
TARN

WASDALE
FELL

LINGMELL BECK

SPRINKLING
TARN

WASDALE
HEAD

HOTEL

P

CORRIDOR ROUTE

PIERS
GILL

GREAT
END
910m

ROAD

GOAT
CRAGS

LINGMELL

LINGMELL
COLL

BROAD
CRAG

P

BROWN
TONGUE

LINGMELL GILL

WASDALE ROUTE

WASDALE ROUTE

WASDALE ROUTE

ROCK
OUT
CROP

SCAFELL
PIKE
978m

WASTWATER

WOOD

N

WOOD

SCAFELL
964m

2 ROUTES TO
SCAFELL PIKE

NOT TO SCALE

TO ESKDALE

SCAFELL PIKE - via Wasdale Head

Approach on the undulating road alongside Wastwater. A sign points to Wasdale Head. Turn right over the stone packhorse bridge. A car park (charge) is at the side of the campsite at the end of Wastwater *(plate 9)*. Your ascent of Scafell Pike begins here. A compass bearing from the car park looking directly to Scafell Pike is 98° magnetic.

Turn left out of the car park. Cross over a cattle grid then cross a wooden bridge where the beck flows into Wastwater 100m to the right. Turn left where a small wooden sign points to Eskdale, then up the right side of the beck.

Near the cottage another small sign says 'Permissive Path, Scafell' which passes the left side of the cottage.

About 100m past the cottage there is another bridge for walkers only, which crosses the small stream. *(plate 10)*. Cross, then go through a gate, follow the path up to the right.

A sign states 'National Trust Property' and is next to a kissing gate. Go through onto a narrow path, this is stony in places, winding it's way up the mountain between the bracken on your left and the beck on your right. The path ascends steeply in places and numerous large rocks cover the path *(plate 11)*.

Looking back you can see Wastwater and the Irish Sea in the background beyond Workington Power Station *(plate 11)*. Scafell Pike is the sheer cliffs you can see directly ahead at the top of the

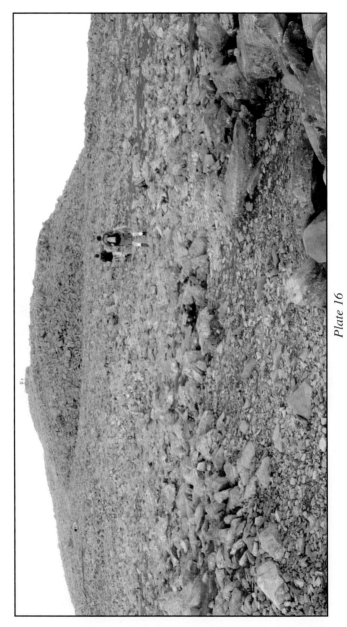

Plate 16
The final approach to Scaffel Pike.

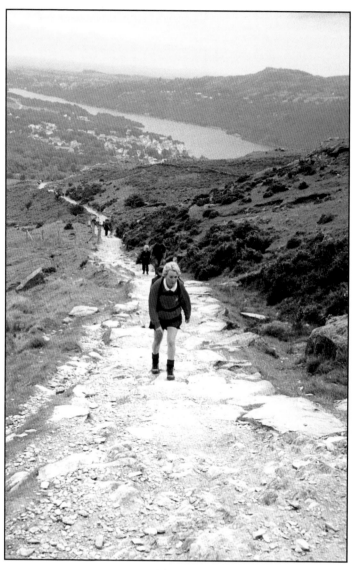

Plate 17
View of Llyn Padarn or Llanberis Lake with the
Llanberis path in the foreground.

valley *(plate 9)*. Pass through another kissing gate with the beck still on the right. Continue up the very stony path.

A compass bearing taken just before Brown Tongue and in direct line to the Pike reads 98°M. You now come to a section of man made cobbled path which is easier to walk on. You can now see Brown Tongue where you ascend the right side *(plate 12)*. There is another section of cobbled path with a pile of stones formed into a cairn.

You now cross the beck at the foot of Brown Tongue, you will see the path across the far side of the beck *(plate 12)*. Ascend the cobbled path alongside another beck.

A small cairn marks a fork in the path, take the left path into heather and peat. The path turns stony soon after. You can see the path ahead but in parts it is not so well defined *(plate 13)*. The ground is flatter here with grass and lots of stones scattered around.

There is a scree slope leading to Mickledore to the right between the Pike and Scafell itself. It is a shorter route to the top but more dangerous to ascend or descend the scree slope, especially at night.

Small cairns mark the main path which is small stone and shale with grass on both sides. There is a stone outcrop to the left side of the Pike *(plate 13)*. Skirt around the left side of it, look for small cairns. Walk in a semi-circle to the large stone outcrop, look carefully to the right for the cairns on the final ascent to the Pike.

Much of the remaining section consists of large stones which you must walk over *(plate 16)*. One slip and you could break an ankle between the stones, so take care here. Look to your left as you ascend, you should see Sty Head Tarn which is near to the beginning of the Corridor Route to Scafell Pike from Seathwaite. Beyond this tarn is Derwent Water *(plate 15)*.

On gaining the summit *(plate 16)* there is a triangulation pillar and a wind shelter. Views from the summit include the Scottish Borders, Blackpool, Windermere and on a clear night the lights of Douglas on the Isle of Man can be seen.

On this as on any mountain peak it can be very cold with gale force winds. The wind chill factor should be taken seriously, so windproof clothing needs to be worn before reaching the summit.

On the return journey down the mountain pick out the path carefully especially in the dark. In the event of low cloud or loss of bearings, follow the bad visibility descent detailed in this book. On a dark clear night the reflection of Wastwater is usually very evident and should help to point you in the general direction of Wasdale Head.

Plate 18
The ridge of Crib Goch with the Pyg track in centre and Miners track at the bottom showing descent from the Pyg track to the Miners track

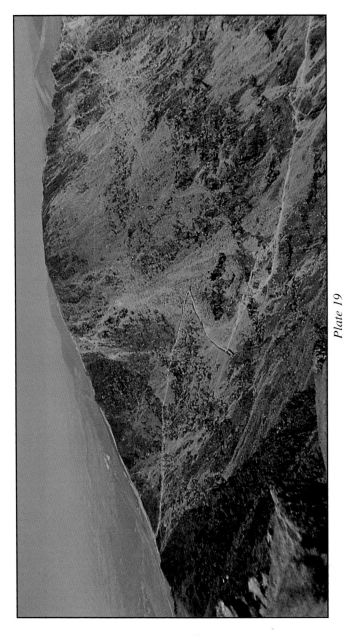

Plate 19

View of the final section of the Pyg track to the Monolith on Snowdon Ridge, showing zig-zag path.

SCAFELL PIKE - via Seathwaite, (Corridor Route)

When you arrive at Seathwaite there is parking available near the farm. Nearby is a small café and a trout farm. Your ascent via the Corridor Route to Scafell Pike starts here.

As you start walking you go through a farm gate, continue on the path. Follow the path going over a stile next to a gate, into the distance up the valley. Cross a small wooden bridge over the river. The path starts to ascend as you go into the head of the valley. Following the course of the stream you come to a gate and stile. The path is undulating.

Cross the small but impressive stone packhorse bridge which is in front. When you pass through the gate the path starts to ascend steeply. Go through a small gate between a stone wall, the obvious path bears off to the right.

Looking back at night towards Seathwaite you can often see a small light at the farm. This is a guide for any walkers returning at night by this route, especially in bad weather.

Approaching the head of the valley the path flattens a little. A waterfall runs on your right and the path becomes very uneven and turns slightly left between the head of the two hills. It is very important to keep the beck on your right because in extreme weather conditions there is a tendency to walk to the higher ground on the left then cross the beck onto the right side which is damp and boggy.

The path along by the beck is very uneven with large stones and is difficult to walk over. There is a cairn on the level area between the two hills. It may be surrounded by water in extreme conditions but is a good route marker. The cairn is approximately 80m from the wooden bridge you see in front following the rough uneven path. Cross the bridge.

The path is now on the right of the beck. In bad conditions it can be very wet. Walk up between the hills to another cairn on your left. Just past it cross the beck again still following the main path. There is a tarn on your left side called Sty Head Tarn *(plate 15)*. Cross over another beck, the path is now better to walk on.

The path starts to divide nearing the head of the valley, it is important to head for the large rocks you see in front of you, the path in parts here is grass. You come to a mountain rescue first aid stretcher box.

To this point the paths are reasonably obvious to see and follow but from here the route becomes difficult to see, walk along and navigate. Take great care and constantly refer to map and compass.

Past the big stone you bear left descending slightly and crossing over some marshy ground. You then rise up again over a grass area then drop down to the foot of the mountain which is straight in front of you. A bearing of 150°M from the stretcher box should take you across and up the side of the mountain along the Corridor Route.

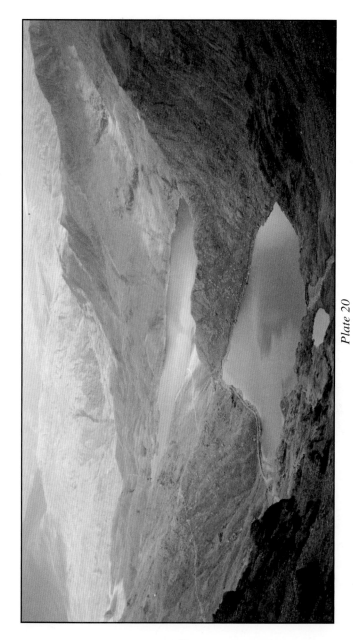

Plate 20
View to Llyn Llydaw reservoir showing Pyg track on left and Miners track around reservoir.

Plate 21
Final approach with steep ascent to the monolith then the summit

Pick up a distinct path up the hillside which is very steep in places with a drop off to your right. Looking down the valley you can see Wastwater. The path winds it's way to the summit but first it leads down and around to the left where there is a small cairn. The area is extremely steep and CARE should be taken. Go around the side of the waterfall known as Piers Gill. You pass another small cairn and some large rocks which you walk between as you near the summit.

On the path there is a ravine with a waterfall. You need to be careful where you are stepping. There is another distinct waterfall coming over the edge on the right with a steep drop down. Keep in to the left side of the path.

You emerge at the foot of Scafell Pike at the base of Lingmell Col. The remaining section has large stones to walk over. Take care not to loose your footing, look for piles of stones marking the route to the summit.

It is left to you the reader to decide which route to choose. I prefer to walk up and return on the Wasdale/Wastwater route. This route is probably better for those who are not extremely skilled in map reading and using a compass. The Corridor Route is not recommended at night and especially in bad conditions. Once on the summit, if conditions are bad, follow the bad visibility descent detailed in this book.

DRIVING ROUTE TO SNOWDON

	Road	Destination
Leave Car Park	**Minor**	Santon Bridge
at Stanton Bridge	**Minor**	Holmrook
at Holmrook	**A595**	Broughton in Furness
at Broughton	**A5092**	Haverthwaite
at Haverthwaite	**A590**	J36 of M6
J36 of M6	**M6**	M56 Chester
M56	**M56**	Queensferry A494
at Queensferry	**A55**	Llandudno Junction
at Llandudno J'tion	**A470**	Betws-y-Coed
at Betws-y-Coed	**A5**	Capel Curig
at Capel Curig	**A4086**	Pass of Llanberis

Park in the main car park at Pen-y-Pass near the youth hostel (charge).

The distance by road is approximately 500miles from Fort William, depending on which driving route you choose. Total drive time is about 10½ hours. It is recommended that drivers be changed regularly to avoid driver fatigue. Care should be taken to observe the speed limits. It is better to reach your destination intact than not at all.

Plate 22

View showing the Pyg track mid left and miners track near the water. Both meet then ascend to summit.

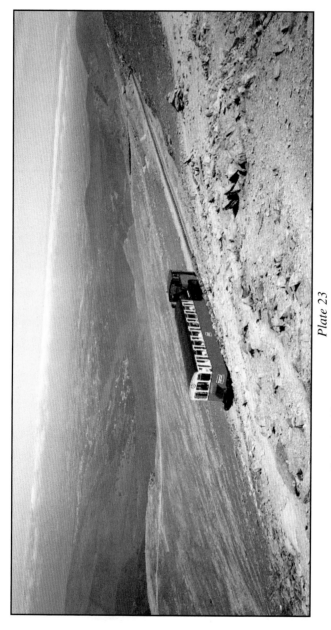

Plate 23
Snowdon Mountain Railway with Llanberis in background

SNOWDON AREA

Mount Snowdon is situated in the Snowdonia National Park, covering an area of 840 square miles. The area around Snowdon is very mountainous as you would imagine. The views all around the region are good and there are some picturesque villages within a short travelling distance.

The main recommended route is situated in the pass of Llanberis where it meets with Pen-y-Pass. There is a youth hostel here and a mountain rescue post. Near Pen-y-Pass there are a number of small lakes or tarns. The largest Llyn Llydaw is a reservoir *(plate 20)*.

The town of Llanberis is 6 miles away on the shore of Llyn Padarn or Llanberis Lake. Along the shore of this lake is a steam railway which is open to visitors. Probably the most famous tourist attraction in this area is the Snowdon Mountain Railway. This line starts in Llanberis and continues to the summit of Snowdon.

On the summit there is a café and gift shop. Thirsty walkers can quench their thirst and purchase souvenirs. Some walkers prefer to travel one way on the railway and the other on foot.

Throughout the area there are many tourist attractions but to do justice to them you need to spend a number of days exploring, walking and visiting all that the Snowdon area has to offer (see section on attractions). A few miles away are Betws-y-Coed and Caernarfon which are worth a visit.

70

SNOWDON

There are 2 main starting points to climb Snowdon on the 3 Peaks Walk. The Pyg Track is the easiest and most popular, the other is the Llanberis Path which ascends from the village of Llanberis.

Start A - The Pyg Track

Park at Pen-y-Pass car park opposite the youth hostel near the top of Llanberis Pass. This car park can be very busy, there is a charge for parking. Your ascent of Snowdon begins here.

Your path is in the upper right hand corner of the car park, continue on the path to a stone wall with an opening between. There are good views from here down the valley. You will see the narrow slate path in front of you. The path ascends a hill, it is very uneven with slabs of stone formed into steps. You can see the obvious path winding up the mountain, keep to this undulating path.

You come to some posts and a wire fence, there are good views of Crib Goch and a reservoir can be seen in the valley. As you look down in the valley you will see the Miners Track which is the alternative route back *(plate 20)*.

A slate chipping path winds round Crib Goch Coll. It starts to ascend as you are walking parallel with the small reservoir, you then look into the next part of the valley as you come over the coll. There is another small tarn in view, tucked into the valley floor *(plate 20)*. The path is very evident into the next part of the valley *(plate 18)*, directly across is Snowdon.

A large expanse of stone, sloping to your left is in front of you, this can be very slippy when wet, boots are advised. You have a good view of the second tarn in front. When you round a large expanse of rock you see the third section of this path which is undulating.

There are veins of quartz in much of the rock formations, these look like snow from a distance. There are the occasional pile of stones on route. As you pass a cairn on your left the path is again scree.

Near the head of the valley is a small pool of water some 30m wide. About 70m further up there is part of a disused quarry on your left, the path bears off to the right.

The ascent now is steeper with a lot of loose stones and shale. You will see a monolith directly ahead of the zig-zag route *(plate 19)*. At the head of this section there are large stone blocks to walk up. *(plate 21)*. Although still ascending, the going is a little easier. From the summit ridge a water pipeline at the bottom of the valley can be seen.

The view once you attain the ridge looking towards Llanberis and in all directions is spectacular *(plate 20 & 22)*. At the monolith you turn left joining the Llanberis Path for the final ascent. The path for the remaining distance to the summit is obvious, it runs parallel with the Snowdon Mountain Railway *(plate 23)*. As you approach you will see the café with the triangulation pillar above, left.

You can go to the triangulation pillar for the customary photograph and viewing session. In the café there is time to relax over a variety of food and drinks while you look out and admire the views. A souvenir shop is next to the café.

You may wish to return to Pen-y-Pass via the Miners Track. This route takes you initially on a steep descent after leaving the Pyg Track *(plate 18)* then is virtually flat for much of the way back before becoming undulating in the last part. The return to Pen-y-Pass by this route is as follows:-

Retrace your steps to the monolith, go down the zig-zag path *(plate 19)*. Just past this you should see a stone/scree descent *(plate 18)* off to your right leading to Glaslyn Tarn. Follow this path to the bottom taking extreme care. Once at the bottom follow the well made track around the reservoir passing some ruined buildings on your left. Go over the causeway and past another tarn. This path will take you back to Pen-y-Pass.

This route is an enjoyable walk and takes approximately 1½ hours to return.

Start B - Llanberis Path

Park your vehicle in Llanberis and walk to the Royal Victoria Hotel near to the Snowdon Mountain Railway. Opposite there are a number of tourist signs. One points to Snowdon Path. Follow this along the road passing a row of houses. Cross the cattle grid at the far end and ascend the very steep metalled road to a holiday house just round a sharp bend. Continue through a metal swing gate onto a stone/shale path, still ascending steeply, to a sign pointing to Snowdon through a metal gate.

Ascend an obvious rough path. The first third ascends steeply as does the last third. This also has a lot of loose stone on it making walking difficult. The central section is on a slight ascent *(plate 17)*.

On the way up you pass under 2 small bridges carrying the Snowdon Mountain Railway. Throughout the summer you may see the trains going up and down the line. You pass a steel structure which was abandoned due to legal disputes during building. This is known as the halfway house and is a convenient refreshment stop being approximately halfway to the summit.

Stay on the obvious path right to the summit. The top half of the route is very exposed in wet and windy weather. Nearing the summit you come to a large stone monolith on your left. This is where the Pyg Track and Miners Track join in a final ascent to the summit *(plate 22)*.

Retrace your steps to return to Llanberis or alternatively descend on one of the other paths.

In the event of lost bearings or low cloud on the summit of Snowdon then follow the bad visibility descent to take you to safer ground.

Now you have conquered all 3 peaks of Scotland, England and Wales you can complete your challenge by driving to Caernarfon and touching the sea.

SLIEVE DONARD – Northern Ireland

Situated - In the Mourne Mountains in the east.

Height – 850 metres

Grid Ref J 357277

How to get there –
Ferry from – Stranraer   Tel: 0870 5707070
                Liverpool Tel: 028 9077 9090
                Troon   Tel: 0870 552 3523

Air to – Belfast City Airport tel: 028 9045 7745
            Belfast International Airport
            Tel: 028 9442 2888

Bus from – Belfast Europa Bus Station
              Tel: 028 3026 3531

Kilkeel Tourist Information – for any further
information you may require
28 Bridge St., Kilkeel, N. Ireland. BT34 4AD

B&B's
Fir Trees, Mrs Donnan, 16 Killowen Old Rd,
Rostrevor, BT34 3AD Tel: 028 4173 8602

Glenbeigh, Mr. Parr, 18 Victoria Sq, Rostrevor,
BT34 3EU   Tel: 028 4173 8281 / 028 4173 8025

Others may be available by contacting the TIC

Heights of Surrounding Peaks –
Slieve Commedagh 767m
Slieve Beg 590m
Slieve Corragh 640m

SLIEVE DONARD - The Route

Start in Donard car park GR.374305, walking from the rear of the car park, stay on the right of the Glen River. Walk through Donard Wood where the path ascends for 150m to Donard Bridge.

Cross the bridge to the left side of the river and walk for 400m to the next bridge, which you cross to take you to the other side again. Continue for 400m to a third bridge and 150m past it is a stile where the open area starts. It takes approx. one hour from here to the summit.

Continue on the obvious track and cross the river where it narrows. The path ascends steeply now for 500m, with a granite causeway up to the Mourne Wall. At this point Slieve Donard comes into full view and you can follow the wall to both Slieve Donard and Slieve Commedagh.

Ascend by the wall to the summit and return by the same route. The views from the summit are spectacular and include the Scottish mountains, Isle of Man, Mountains of NW England and Snowdonia in Wales.

Even though this mountain is the smallest out of the four, it can be very cold and inhospitable on the summit so if you do intend to walk the 4th peak, ensure you go properly prepared.

BAD VISIBILITY DESCENTS

During the ascent of any mountain care should be taken especially in bad visibility.

More accidents happen on the return journey than on the ascent. It may be difficult to pick out the path of descent in low cloud or in darkness. In situations like this follow the bearings and details below to ensure a safe descent from the summit.

Ben Nevis

Walk from the triangulation pillar on a **Grid Bearing** of **225°** for **100m. Caution - Do Not Veer to the Right!**

Follow a **Grid Bearing** of **224°** for **60m,** which should take you clear of the plateau onto your path.

Approx. **Grid Bearing 280°** for 700m follow winding path. Stay on path; **do not take bearing more than 281°**

Magnetic North is estimated at 3° W of Grid North in July 2003 this decreases by about ½° every four years. The compass bearing is gained by adding this difference to the grid bearing, this is known as a magnetic bearing. Refer to current O.S. maps for magnetic variation.

Scafell Pike

Walk from the triangulation pillar on a **Grid Bearing** of **315°** for **300m**. Look carefully for the path and cairns.

Walk for **200m** on **Grid Bearing 294°**
Walk for **230m** on **Grid Bearing 336°**
Walk on Grid Bearing 231°

From this point follow descending path towards Brown Tongue

This route takes you to the left of Dropping Crag, down to Lingmell Col and left around to Hollow Stones. In this area magnetic north is 3° W of Grid North in 2004. The compass bearing is gained by adding this difference to the grid bearing. Refer to current O.S. maps for magnetic variation.

Following this course from the summit should bring you off the peak and below the rocks in front of the Pike itself. From this point you can follow the path downhill to Wastwater looking for the piles of stones on route.

Snowdon

Walk from the summit station/café on **Grid Bearing 347°** for **500m** following the distinct path. A railway line is on the left and a steep drop on the right. At the monolith turn right on **Grid Bearing 48°.** You are now on another distinct path going downhill. This path zig-zags sharply *(plate 19)*. Stay on this path to descend, eventually leading back to Pen-y-Pass. In extreme bad weather follow the railway line down into Llanberis.

In the event of low cloud or other problem on the top half of the route, the Miners Track will take you to the valley quicker *(plate 18)*. It starts about a third of the way down the mountain and branches off to the right. The path is steep at first but once at the bottom it is a good path to Pen-y-Pass. A sign is situated at the Pen-y-Pass end of this track giving current weather conditions.

In this area magnetic north is 3° W of Grid North in 2005 decreasing by about ½° in four years. The compass bearing is gained by adding the difference to the grid bearing. Refer to current O.S. maps for magnetic variation.

SUPPORT TEAM

When attempting the National 3 Peaks it is advisable to have a support team of 2-4 people who are able to drive between the 3 peaks and provide the food and drinks to tired walkers. **It is not advisable for walkers to both attempt the 3 peaks and drive between each area.** The general tiredness of driving the long distance between each mountain and the walker's fatigue makes it important to have a support team.

Providing food and warm drinks to walkers is very important especially in bad conditions. The last thing walkers need on returning to the foothills of each peak is to start preparing food and drinks. The assistance of a support team is therefore vital.

Members of any support team should have some knowledge of first aid and should be able to recognise the symptoms of exposure. They should be aware of the location of the mountain rescue posts and nearest telephone for emergency. The support team should keep a spare rucksack with the following inside:-

Map	Compass
Whistle	Emergency Food
Survival Bag	Notepad/Pencil
Spare Clothing	First Aid Kit
Matches	

Torch (spare bulb/batteries)
Mobile Telephone (not always guaranteed to function in mountainous areas)

Where possible there should be two of the support team who are experienced and prepared to give assistance to any of the walkers in an accident/emergency situation. It may be decided that initially the best course of action is to go straight to the aid of a walker rather than contact the mountain rescue team. Any potential risks to either the injured or lost walker or the rescuer should be carefully considered before deciding your course of action.

POST WALK

After achieving your goal of walking the National 3 Peaks, whether it is in 24 hours or over a prolonged time, you may like a souvenir to mark the event. The author has produced a selection of 3 Peak items which are for sale. These are exclusive to Challenge Publications and include:- polo/t-shirts, cloth/metal badges, certificates for individual peaks or all 3 peaks and driver/support certificates, also Ben Nevis desk calendars.

Due to low cloud on the summit of one or more peaks, you may not be able to take any photographs. The author has individual CDs for each route, with between 121 – 173 superb photographs of the route up each mountain, with many views from the summits. These will help you prepare for your walk or help you relive your memories. They can be viewed on a PC or on a television via a DVD player. Photographs can be printed from them.

Full details are available for all souvenirs by sending for a current price list enclosing a S.A.E. to:-

Brian Smailes
Challenge Publications
7, Earlsmere Drive
Ardsley
Barnsley
South Yorkshire
S71 5HH

The author is compiling a register of successful attempts and would be pleased to receive names of walkers or any details and/or comments about your walk.

USEFUL INFORMATION

Heights of Peaks

Ben Nevis -1344 metres
Scafell Pike- 978 metres
Snowdon   - 1085 metres

Nearest Main Towns

Ben Nevis - Fort William
Scafell Pike- Keswick
Snowdon   - Llanberis

Nearest Telephone

Ben Nevis - Beside Glen Nevis Youth Hostel
            Glen Nevis Visitor Centre
            Ben Nevis Inn
Scafell   - Wasdale Head Hotel
            - Farms and houses at base of
            Wastwater
            - Seathwaite
Snowdon   - Pen-y-Pass
            - Llanberis
            - Café on Snowdon Summit

Mountain Rescue Posts

Ben Nevis - Fort William town centre
Scafell   - Gatesgarth (Buttermere)
            - Wasdale Head
            - Mountain Rescue Kit near Sty
            Head on the Corridor Route
Snowdon   - Pen-y-Pass
            - Nant Peris in Pass of Llanberis

Recommended Maps

Ben Nevis - O.S. Explorer No. 392
Ben Nevis & Fort William (1:25,000)

Scafell - O.S. Explorer No. OL4
English Lakes (1:25,000)
- O.S. Explorer No. OL6
English Lakes (1:25,000)

Snowdon - O.S. Explorer No. OL17
Snowdonia (1:25,000)

Weatherline Information

Ben Nevis Area   01397 705922
Scafell Area   017687 75757
Snowdon Area   09068 500449
General Weather Web site
www.metoffice.gov.uk
(click on mountain weather)

Grid References

Ben Nevis

Glen Nevis Visitor Centre   G.R. 122729
Glen Nevis Youth Hostel   G.R. 128718
Halfway point on main path, near Lochan
Lochan Meall An t-Suidhe   G.R. 147724
Emergency shelter, Ben Nevis summit
G.R. 168712

Beware, other shelters on Carn Dearg and
Coire Leis have been removed (Oct 2004)

Scafell Pike

Wastwater, Wasdale Head car park
G.R. 181076
Base of Scafell Pike   G.R. 207074
Scafell Pike summit   G.R. 215072
Sty Head Tarn, Corridor Rte. G.R. 221099
Seathwaite car park, Corridor Rte.
G.R. 235422

Snowdon

Pen-y-Pass car park   G.R. 647556
Start of Llanberis Path   G.R. 581595
Snowdon summit   G.R. 610544

Timing for each mountain

Ben Nevis

Visitor Centre start to summit $3\frac{3}{4}$ hours
Summit to Visitor Centre $2\frac{3}{4}$ hours
Youth Hostel start to summit $3\frac{3}{4}$ hours
Summit to youth hostel $2\frac{3}{4}$ hours

Scafell Pike

Wasdale Head start to summit $2\frac{1}{2}$ hours
Summit to Wasdale Head $2\frac{1}{4}$ hours
Seathwaite, start to summit $3\frac{1}{2}$ hours

Snowdon

Pen-y-Pass, Pyg Track start
to summit $2\frac{1}{4}$ hours
Summit to Pen-y-Pass,
via Miners Track $1\frac{3}{4}$ hours
Llanberis Path to summit $2\frac{1}{2}$ hours
Summit to Llanberis $1\frac{3}{4}$ hours

These timings will vary depending on the skill and fitness of your party and weather conditions e.g. Ben Nevis can be completed in 4½ hours with ease.

Suggested Itinerary

24 Hours Challenge

        4 pm touch water - Fort William
        4.30pm start base of Ben Nevis
        6.45pm summit of Ben Nevis
        8.30pm base of Ben Nevis
        2am start base of Scafell Pike
        4.45am summit of Scafell Pike
        6.15am base of Scafell Pike
        12.30pm start base of Snowdon
        2.30pm summit of Snowdon
        3.30pm base of Snowdon
        4pm touch water - Caernarfon

A Weekend Challenge

        Saturday
        start   2am   Glen Nevis Visitor Centre
                 5.45am   Ben Nevis summit
                 8.30am   Glen Nevis Visitor Centre
                 4 30pm   Seathwaite-Lake District
                 8pm   Scafell Pike summit
                 10.15pm Wasdale Head
        Sunday
                 8am   Pen-y-Pass-Snowdon
                 10.15pm Snowdon summit
        finish   12.30pm Sunday Pen-y-Pass car park

National Park/Tourist Information Centres

Glen Nevis Visitor Centre	01397 705922
Fort William T.I.C. Information Line	0845 2255121
Ballachulish TIC	01855 811296
Kingdom of Scotland Visitor Centre	
Spean Bridge	01397 712999

Keswick Information Centre	017687 72645
Seatoller Barn Info. Centre	017687 77294

Llanberis T.I.C.	01286 870765
Betws-y-Coed	01690 710426
Caernarfon	01286 672232

Taxi Service in Fort William Area
Jenny Keane - Clansman Taxis 01397 703334

This accommodation in each area is not arranged in any order of priority. All are within as reasonable distance to the walking routes as possible.

Accommodation-Ben Nevis area

Campsite
Glen Nevis Caravan & Camping Park 01397 702191
Glen Nevis, Fort William

Youth Hostel
Glen Nevis Youth Hostel   01397 702336
Glen Nevis

Ben Nevis Inn (Bunkhouse)   01397 701227
Achintee, By Claggan, Fort William PH33 6TE
info@ben-nevis-inn.co.uk
www.ben-nevis-inn.co.uk

Self Catering Caravans/Chalets

Margaret Ferguson   01397 705905
'Harland'
Glen Nevis
Fort William PH33 6ST
ferguson@glennevis1.freeserve.co.uk

Bed & Breakfast

Constantia House,   01397 702893
Fassifern Road,
Fort William. PH33 6BD
derek.walker61@btinternet.com

Craig Nevis Guest House   01397 702023
Belford Road
Fort William. PH33 6BU
craigdon42@hotmail.com

Corrie Duff Guest House & Holiday Cottages
Corrie Duff   01397 701412
Glen Nevis
Fort William.PH33 6ST
corrie@corrieduff.fsnet.co.uk

'Glenfer'   01397 705848
Glen Nevis
Fort William. PH33 6PF
stay@glenfer.co.uk   www.glenfer.co.uk

Accommodation-Scafell Area

Campsites

Seathwaite Farm   017687 77394
Wasdale Head, Barn Door Shop-
          (no showers)   019467 26384
Wasdale Head (Nat.Trust site)   019467 26220

Youth Hostels

Wasdale Hall Youth Hostel   019467 26222
Borrowdale Youth Hostel   017687 77257

Bed & Breakfast

Seathwaite Farm Cottage
Seathwaite, Borrowdale, Keswick
Cumbria. CA12 5XJ   017687 77284

Gillian Race   019467 26242
Burnthwaite Farm
Wasdale Head, Seascale
Cumbria. CA20 1EX
burnthwaite123@aol.com

Accommodation-Snowdon Area

Campsite

Ty Isaf, Nant Peris   01286 870494

Youth Hostels

Pen-y-Pass   0870 7705990
Capel Curig   0870 7705746
Llanberis   0870 7705928

Bed & Breakfast

Bron-y-Graig,   01286 872073
Capel Coch, Llanberis LL55 4SH
www.bronygraig.com   brickaby@onetel.com

Erw Fair   01286 872400
High Street
Llanberis LL55 4HA
www.erwfair.com   erwfair@fsmail.net

Attractions in each Area

Ben Nevis Area

Crannog Cruises	01397 700714
Nevis Range Cable Cars	01397 705825
Ben Nevis Distillery	01397 702476
Ben Nevis Highland Centre	01397 704244
West Highland Museum	01397 702169
Lochaber Leisure Centre	01397 704359

Scafell Area

Keswick Launch on Derwentwater	017687 72263
Motor Museum, Keswick	017687 73757
Cumberland Pencil Museum	017687 73626
'The Theatre by the Lake' Keswick	017687 74411

Snowdon Area

Snowdon Mountain Railway	0870 458 0033
Electric Mountain	01286 870636
Llanberis Lake Railway	01286 870549
Padarn Country Park	01286 870892

Taxi Service in Fort William Area

Jenny Keane - Clansman Taxis 01397 703334

Useful Addresses/Tel No's

Long Distance Walkers Association
Paul Lawrence,
15, Tamarisk Rise,
Wokingham,
Berkshire RG40 1WG
Tel: 01189 790190
This association is set up to further the interests of those who enjoy long distance walking. Members receive a journal three times each year, which includes information on all aspects of long distance walking.

Ramblers Association
2nd Floor, Camelford House,
87-90 Albert Embankment,
London SE1 7TW
Tel: 01577 861222
Advice and information on all walking matters. Local groups with regular meetings.

Scottish Natural Heritage
www.snh.org.uk

The Countryside Agency for England
www.countryside.gov.uk/access

The Countryside Council for Wales
www.ccw.gov.uk

Rail services to Fort William
www.scotrail.co.uk   08457 48 49 50

Public Transport Information for Fort William
0870 608 2 608

The routes described in this book were used by the author in 2004 and believed to be correct at the time of publication. Hopefully you have enjoyed your 3 peaks adventure and gained as much pleasure from walking the route as he did. Should you wish to walk other challenging routes, please visit Challenge Publications website at: -

www.chall-pub.fsnet.co.uk

On our website you will find other interesting, and possibly different walks around the British Isles, which are equally as picturesque and enjoyable as this one.

Should you wish to comment on this book or give further information to help keep the book updated then please write to the address below or e-mail via the website. An acknowledgement will be given: -

Please write to: -
Challenge Publications
7, Earlsmere Drive,
Ardsley,
Barnsley.
S71 5HH

GLOSSARY OF WORDS

Bearing - *A degree or number of degrees set on a compass, follow the direction of travel arrow walking on that bearing to reach your intended destination.*

Beck - *Cumbrian word for stream or brook.*

Burn - *Scottish word meaning stream, brook, beck or watercourse.*

Cairn - *An ancient stone mound erected as a marker. Often modern day piles of stones that denote a path or route are referred to as cairns.*

Col - *A pass or saddle between two hills. It provides access between one valley and another.*

Crag - *A steep rugged rock or peak.*

Escape Route - *Used for any emergency situation or in times of bad visibility. The main aim is to get you down to lower ground by the safest and quickest way.*

Glen - *Scottish word for a valley.*

Grid Reference - *Derived from the national grid reference system. This is used to pinpoint a place on a map by use of letters and numbers.*

Gully - *A narrow channel or cleft in a rock face, may have waterfalls and can be very slippery and have vertical drops.*

Kissing Gate - *Swing gate that usually lets one person through it at a time by moving the gate backwards and forwards.*

Loch - *Scottish word for lake.*

Magnetic Bearing - *This is a grid bearing taken from a map and the relevant magnetic variation added to it to obtain the magnetic bearing. See the relevant maps for details of current magnetic variation.*

Metalled Road - *Generally known as a stone chipping road. This term evolved and became regarded as the roads metal or the roads surface.*

Outcrop - *Part of a rock formation that sticks out from the main body of rock.*

Path - *A walk way or route under two metres wide.*

Plateau - *A wide and mainly flat area of elevated land.*

Route Card - *A plan of action prepared before you leave. A copy to be left with someone so that if you fail to return by a planned time then help can be summoned.*

Summit - *The highest point of a mountain or hill.*

Tarn - *A small mountain lake.*

Track - *A route more than two metres wide.*

Trig Point - *True name is Triangulation Pillar. These mark the summit of many mountains but not all. It is a small stone pillar with a number on it. The height of the mountain is taken from this point.*